Towards a Quantitative Assessment of Aid for Trade

Massimiliano Calì
Dirk Willem te Velde

COMMONWEALTH SECRETARIAT

Commonwealth Secretariat
Marlborough House, Pall Mall
London SW1Y 5HX, United Kingdom

Economic Paper 83 in the Commonwealth Economic Paper Series

The authors are affiliated to the Overseas Development Institute, London.

Published by the Commonwealth Secretariat
Edited and designed by Wayzgoose
Cover design by Tattersall Hammarling and Silk
Printed by Hobbs the Printers Ltd, Totton, Hampshire

Copies of this publication may be obtained from

The Publications Section
Commonwealth Secretariat, Marlborough House
Pall Mall, London SW1Y 5HX
United Kingdom
Tel: +44 (0)20 7747 6534
Fax: +44 (0)20 7839 9081
Email: publications@commonwealth.int
Web: www.thecommonwealth.org/publications

A catalogue record for this publication is available from the British Library.

ISBN: 978-0-85092-889-1 (paperback)
ISBN: 978-1-84859-019-9 (downloadable e-book)

Contents

Acronyms and abbreviations

ACP	African Caribbean Pacific (countries)
AfT	Aid for Trade
CRS	Credit Reporting System
GDP	Gross Domestic Product
GNI	Gross National Income
GNP	Gross National Product
IF	Integrated Framework
LDC	Least Developed Country
ODI	Overseas Development Institute
OECD	Organisation for Economic Co-operation and Development
OLS	Ordinary Least Squares
REER	Real Effective Exchange Rate
RTA	Regional Trade Agreement
WTO	World Trade Organization

Summary

Aid for Trade (AfT) has moved up both the aid and trade agendas. There is now a need for quantitative evidence which can be used to identify needs and inform an analysis of how AfT can best be provided.

The WTO Aid for Trade Task Force has identified six categories of AfT and builds upon the definitions used in the WTO/OECD trade-related and capacity building database (WTO database). They are: trade policy and regulations; trade development; trade-related infrastructure; building productive capacity (including private sector development); trade-related adjustment (including support for adjustment associated with changes in international trade regimes); and other trade-related needs. The aim of this study is to increase understanding of whether and how AfT can help developing countries to trade and improve their economic performance.

Section 2 discusses expected pathways of the effects of AfT. If it is used effectively, AfT can have a positive effect on trade by tackling both market and governance failures. It can:

- Improve trade policy co-ordination (*AfT category:* trade development);
- Develop standards to improve access for exports (*AfT category:* trade facilitation);
- Improve skill formation (*AfT category:* trade-related adjustment);
- Improve infrastructure (*AfT category:* trade-related infrastructure);
- Overcome governance failures, such as weak institutions or weak administrative procedures (*AfT category:* trade policy and rules).

The paper uses statistical evidence to examine the effects of AfT on the costs of trading and the level of exports. It goes beyond previous evidence on the effects of aid, and in particular of AfT, on trade. It examines specific aid categories and sectoral relationships. AfT reduces the costs of trading, an important investment climate indicator and one which is particularly relevant for importing and exporting. This result holds when controlling for other factors affecting trade costs, such as governance generally, being landlocked and income status. For a sample of 120 developing countries, it is estimated that an increase of 1 per cent in AfT (for trade policy and regulations) leads to a fall of approximately 0.15 per cent in the cost of exporting. Thus, an increase of US$15,000 (from the mean of US$1.48 million) is associated with a reduction of US$1.80 (from the mean of US$1324) in the cost of packing goods and loading them into a 20-foot container, transporting them to the port of departure and loading them on a vessel or truck.

Aid for trade fosters exports, although the relationship is non-linear and the effect depends on a careful specification of the types of aid and exports, in line with existing literature on aid. We model aid to productive capacities by sector, while the effects of aid to infrastructure depend on empirical specifications. The paper uses a new estimation identification strategy based on inter-sectoral and intra-sectoral (over time) differences in exports and AfT. It divides aid to productive capacities into aid to the different sectors and then correlates sectoral aid to sectoral exports. The identification of AfT effects comes from analysing whether sectors that receive more aid relative to other sectors in the same country experience relatively faster growth in their exports, as well as whether exports of a sector grow faster in years in which that sector receives relatively higher levels of aid. The main advantage of this strategy is that it allows control for all time varying country factors which may influence exports, such as effective demand, policies, size of the economy, economic fundamentals and country-level shocks. The results based on this new identification strategy are clear: they show that aid has a robust, positive and non-linear effect on productive capacities in relation to exports.

1

Background and Motivation

Aid for Trade has moved up both the aid and trade agendas. Several studies have described the rationale for AfT, but it is now time to move beyond the descriptive stage and analyse the needs and design its implementation. A key motivation behind the research presented in this paper is that there is a lack of good quantitative evidence on:

1. Actual AfT flows in-country;[1] and
2. The possible effects of AfT.[2]

This study is designed to provide an understanding of whether and how AfT can help developing countries trade and improve their economic performance. It also illustrates the scope and limitations of a quantitative approach towards AfT, and should be read in conjunction with a study of whether AfT flows can actually be measured (Turner, 2008).

The paper discusses the effects of AfT. There are two ways of defining the scope of this question. The first is to focus on the Aid for Trade initiative adopted by the WTO during the Doha negotiations. This now has legal status as a WTO agreement. Specifically, the Aid for Trade Task Force argued that developing countries 'expect Aid-for-Trade to go well beyond the scope of the IF' (WTO, 2006). The Integrated Framework (IF) performs trade diagnostics rather than supporting productive capacities or infrastructure. The Task Force identified six categories of AfT and builds upon the definitions used in the WTO/OECD trade-related and capacity building database:[3]

- Trade policy and regulations;
- Trade development;
- Trade-related infrastructure;
- Building productive capacity (including private sector development);
- Trade-related adjustment (including support for adjustment associated with changes in international trade regimes);
- Other trade-related needs.

On this definition, AfT contributes to the provision of governance public goods, such as trade rules (to help countries implement and benefit from multilateral trade liberalisation) and regional public goods, such as cross-border infrastructure facilities (to facilitate intra-regional trade). Such effects could be measured by volume of funds and the emergence of new cross-border initiatives such as corridor approaches.

However, this focuses on a different way of examining the effects of aid for trade (lower case). This approach recognises that donor countries were already providing this form of aid long before the Aid for Trade (upper case) label was introduced. Therefore, we should be able to address whether aid for trade has any impact using historical data on trade-related aid, as collected by the OECD. (This is, of course, subject to the reliability of reporting by donors to the OECD.)

The paper is organised as follows. Section 2 examines how AfT is expected to affect trade, growth and economic performance more generally. Section 3 suggests an empirical framework and describes the data used to test the theoretical hypotheses. Section 4 provides new empirical results. Section 5 sets out the policy implications and suggests directions for future research.

2

The Effectiveness of Aid for Trade

Expected pathways

We first discuss why certain types of aid should produce particular effects on trade, so that we can propose hypotheses and assess the relevance of empirical patterns in the context of Aid for Trade. Table 2.1 identifies potential market and governance failures affecting the development of trade and suggests policy responses to address these failures. It identifies whether a proposed response could be assisted by an AfT package and what part of the package would be relevant to the task (on the basis of its current classification in the OECD Credit Reporting System (CRS) aid statistics).

Table 2.1 suggests that if employed effectively AfT can:

- Improve trade policy co-ordination (*AfT category:* trade development);
- Develop standards to improve access for exports (*AfT category:*trade facilitation);
- Improve skill formation (*AfT category:*trade-related adjustment);
- Improve infrastructure (*AfT category:*trade-related infrastructure);
- Overcome governance failures, such as weak institutions or weak administrative procedures (*AfT category:*trade policy and rules).

AfT also has a number of other more indirect effects. For example, the shift to giving trade priority in aid spending aims to put more emphasis on economic development and the supply side. The share of aid going to economic infrastructure decreased dramatically after a mid-1990s donor consensus that social sectors had to be supported (Figure 2.1).

The actual macroeconomic effects of aid depend on the functioning of a number of channels, e.g. whether the exchange rate appreciates due to inflationary expansion, so that exports decline, or whether aid actually improves trade competitiveness through better infrastructure. From an economic point of view, if more support goes via investment and productive uses, rather than to consumption or other projects with less growth potential, this will help to remove or reduce the Dutch disease effects of increased aid. This is confirmed by Adam and Bevan (2006). They use a computable general equilibrium model to show that aid-funded increases in public investment yield potentially large medium-term welfare gains, as public infrastructure investments offset short-run Dutch disease effects.

We do not have enough information to predict what channels may be relatively more important for trade-related outcomes. Our hypothesis is that both the direct and indirect effects of AfT are potentially important in stimulating competitiveness and exports.

Table 2.1. How Aid for Trade can address market and governance failures

Broad source/ area of failure	Examples of failures	Responses: policies and activities	Role for Aid for Trade?
Market failures			
Co-ordination	Externalities ignored. Linkages not exploited Complementarities not exploited.	Capacity building for trade policy to identify linkages and externalities. National trade strategy	Yes, training and institutional development.
Developing, adapting and adopting technology	Incomplete and imperfect information. Network externalities.	Facilitate technology transfer and adoption. Support for quality control to meet export standards.	Yes, trade facilitation. Assisting co-ordination with the private sector.
Skills formation	Under-investment in training due to inability to appropriate externalities (in training workers) due to imperfect information.	Better co-ordination and/ or subsidies for training. Strengthen information flows.	Mostly not included under AfT. Could be included in trade-related adjustment.
Capital markets Access to finance	Difficult access to credit. High interest rates.	Credit schemes. Formal sector subsidy based on improved information about borrowers.	Normally not included under AfT.
Infrastructure	Lack of good quality infrastructure because lumpy investment gets postponed in uncertain times.	Provide incentives for public-private partnerships. Provide grants in the case of low financial return/high economic return.	Yes, aid to economic infrastructure and better co-ordination with development finance institutions/ private sector.
Governance failure			
Regulatory and administrative structure	Burdensome administrative requirements.	Streamline administrative procedures and regulation.	Yes, trade policy and regulations (especially trade facilitation).

Source: Adapted from Te Velde (2008)

These effects are the product of a complex causality chain running from aid to country outcomes and mediated by domestic policy makers, implementation agencies, policies and country conditions. Bourguignon and Sundberg (2007) define this chain as a 'black-box', as models usually do not include the actual way. 'If a dollar of aid produces little discernible change, was the objective ill-defined, the service delivery inefficient, bureaucratic measures inadequate, or was money diverted?' (Bourguignon and Sundberg (2007, p. 317). This problem applies to our analysis as well, but it is less significant than for models which

Figure 2.1. Share of total aid to economic infrastructure and productive sectors

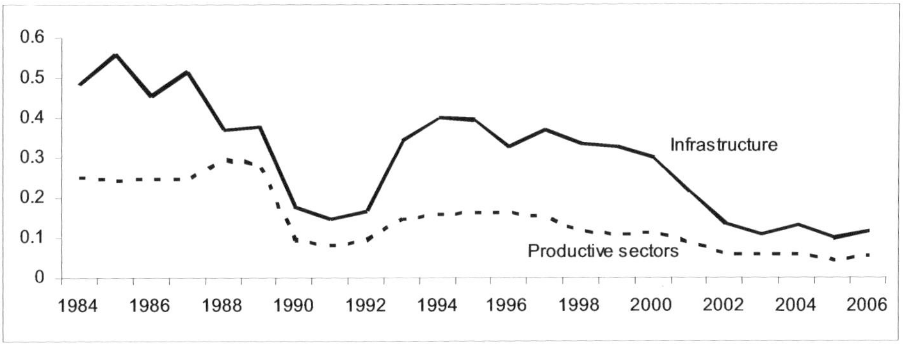

Source: OECD CRS disbursements

estimate a relationship between aid and growth, as here we identify the links between AfT and specific outcomes.

These outcomes can be linked directly to certain types of aid for trade, for example trade-related administrative support, or they can be linked less directly, for example the impact of aid for infrastructure on the values of exports and imports, which are also influenced by many other factors. Moreover, some outcomes can be clearly measurable (e.g. streamlined administrative procedures could be measured through the cost of processing an export), while others are less easily measurable (e.g. improved trade policy co-ordination). We will try to measure the impact of different types of aid for trade on measurable outcomes, direct and indirect.

Empirical literature on aid effectiveness

There is a large empirical literature on the macro relationships between aid, growth and investment, although not specifically on the effects of AfT. This literature tries to investigate the effects of aid on growth on the basis of a neoclassical growth model, where aid provides a boost in capital accumulation and thus to growth.[4] The findings of this literature have been at best mixed, with no consensus on the direction of the effects, let alone on their size.

Consider first the effects of general aid. Burnside and Dollar (2000) argue that aid has no identifiable additional effect on growth once other factors have been accounted for, including economic policies. Aid raises growth only in countries with 'good' policies. Hansen and Tarp (2001) use different econometric specifications and find that aid is effective and that the results do not depend on policy. In a number of recent studies, Rajan and Subramanian (2005; 2007) use longer time spans and show that the impact of aid on growth is less positive. The authors (2005) use an innovative strategy to examine the impact of aid across sectors within one country. In this way, they can better control for omitted variables bias or model specification. Their main finding is that aid has systematic adverse effects on a country's competitiveness, which is reflected in a reduction of the share of labour-intensive and tradable industries in the manufacturing sector. They suggest that these are Dutch disease effects, related to the real exchange rate overvaluation caused by aid inflows. Using a large panel of countries and instrumentation strategy to correct for the bias in conventional OLS estimation, Rajan and Subramanian (2007) do not find any positive relationship between aid and growth.

After analysing 97 different empirical studies on the impact of aid on growth, Doucouliagos and Paldam (2007) conclude that the impact of aid on growth is not significant. A number of factors may explain the inconclusiveness of these research efforts. Bourguignon and Sundberg (2007) argue that these mixed results are not surprising, given the heterogeneity of aid motives and the complex causality chain linking foreign aid to growth. Further, the impact of aid might depend on domestic economic policies, institutions and other conditions. Hansen and Tarp (2001) point to the lack of a satisfactory theoretical framework underpinning the empirical analysis. The simple neoclassical growth model of capital accumulation does not offer a framework to derive an exact empirical specification for a very complex relationship such as the one between aid and growth. Moreover the direction of causality (from aid to growth or vice versa) is to some extent still an unresolved issue.

There are number of studies that disaggregate aid by type or category. McPherson and Rakowski (2001) use a multi-equation system and find that the impact of aid on GDP per capita growth is positive but indirect through investment. Also emphasising that aid affects growth through investment, Gomanee, Girma and Morrissey (2002) find on the basis of 25 sub-Saharan African countriesin the period 1970–1997 that every 1 percentage point in the ratio of aid to GNP contributes one-third of 1 percentage point to growth.

Clemens et al. (2004) split aid into different types and identify the types of aid that could plausibly stimulate growth in the short run. These include budget and balance of payments support, investments in infrastructure and aid for productive sectors. The study finds that this type of aid has a large positive effect on short-term growth: a $1 increase in aid raises the present value of output by $8, although this effect decreases at the margin. These results survive a number of checks for robustness, but they are based on a short time horizon (1997–2001).

A few studies have quantified the effects of infrastructure provision from trade and growth and all find a positive correlation. François and Manchin (2007) estimate a large panel of bilateral trade flows over the period 1988–2002 for a number of countries and focus on the effects of communications and transport infrastructure. They estimate that an increase of one standard deviation (from the mean) in the communications infrastructure raises the volume of trade by roughly 11 per cent, compared to a 7 per cent effect on transport infrastructure and a 2 per cent effect on trade for tariffs. For least developed countries (LDCs), transport is more important than communications. The effects of communications infrastructure on trade grow as a country reaches the middle-income range. Buys et al. (2006) find that upgrading a primary road network connecting the major 83 urban areas in sub-Saharan Africa would expand overland trade within the region by around US$250 billion over 15 years. Other studies have quantified the positive relation between infrastructure and growth, although they have been unable to properly address the problem of causality (e.g. Canning et al., 1994; Canning, 1998). It seems natural to hypothesise that more aid to infrastructure should foster growth and exports.

By focusing our analysis on Aid for Trade, we can depart from the aid-growth conundrum by isolating the impacts of specific types of aid on specific outcomes. The rationale and objectives behind AfT are clearly narrower than those behind general aid and this should allow a more precise identification strategy. We test for the effects of total trade-related aid and specific types of AfT on trade-related outcomes, including the costs of trading and the level of exports.

3

The Effects of Aid for Trade – An Empirical Framework

We use two broad ways of assessing the impact of AfT: its effect on the costs of trading and on exports.

Aid for Trade and the costs of trading

First, we estimate whether particular types of AfT have affected trade costs as measured investment climate indicators at the macro level, such as the time taken by customs to clear imports and exports, and the cost of exporting and importing goods across countries and over time (conditioning on other variables). These variables measure separately the time and the costs (in US$) of handling and transporting a 20-foot container to (or from) the port of departure (or entry). In the case of costs, these include costs for documents, administrative fees for customs clearance and technical control, terminal handling charges and fees for in-country transport. The cost measure does not include tariffs or trade taxes. Only official costs are recorded. These cost and time variables only capture the efficiency with which exports and imports are handled *within* the country of interest. For instance, in the case of exports, procedures start after the goods are packed at the factory and include all official costs until the goods' departure from the point of exit. For imports, procedures start when goods are unloaded from a vessel at the port of entry or when the vehicle carrying them has crossed the border and go on until delivery at the factory or warehouse (see Appendix 1 for a more complete description). Therefore these measures are not affected by the degree of isolation of the country (e.g. its distance from its trading partners), as the costs of transporting the goods from (or to) the point of departure (or destination) are excluded. This analysis is important, as the costs faced and the time taken by firms to trade goods are significant determinants of a country's competitiveness. Djankov et al. (2006) find that each additional day that a product is delayed prior to shipping reduces trade by at least 1 per cent.

The equation we test at the macro level is:

$$\ln(IC)^{Z}_{i,(2008)} = \alpha + \beta_1 \ln(1 + Atpr)_{i,(2006)} + \beta_2 \ln(IC)_{i,(2007)} + \Gamma Z_i + \varepsilon_i \qquad (1)$$

where IC is an investment climate indicator (country i, indicator z), $Atpr_{(2006)}$ is aid for trade policy and regulation (in thousands US$) lagged two years, and Z is a vector of other determinants of IC. We use $\ln(1{+}Atpr)$ to avoid missing and negative values.[5] Specification (1) tests whether this type of aid for trade does indeed determine significant changes in the procedural costs of and the time taken to trade across borders. This is a direct test, as a substantial part of *Atpr* is aimed at reducing the costs of trading across borders.[6] In particular, AfT facilitation is one of the parts of *Atpr* specifically targeting the reduction of these types of costs.

According to the data description by WTO/OECD:

> ... trade facilitation relates to a wide range of activities such as import and export procedures (e.g. customs or licensing procedures); transport formalities; and payments, insurance, and other financial requirements [...] Cutting red tape at the point where goods enter a country and providing easier access to this kind of information are two ways of 'facilitating' trade. WTO/OECD (2008)

We will also test the effects of aid for trade facilitation on *IC* variables.[7] We relate the *IC* variable in 2008 to the aid for trade regressor in 2006, as the former is measured at the beginning of the year to which it refers.

Other investment climate indicators which may also affect trade include variables such as being landlocked, income levels, size of the country and governance indicators from Kaufmann et al. (2007). Kaufmann indicators measure perceptions of the effectiveness of government. Income levels are important because higher levels are associated with better institutions and rules. The size and geographical status of countries clearly affect trade costs.

Aid for Trade and exports

Secondly, we will estimate the effects of AfT on exports directly, using an augmented export demand equation which includes AfT. We need to justify adding (aid to) infrastructure and productive capacities to an export demand equation. Better infrastructure and capabilities should improve productivity and hence prices, which would be reflected in the standard specification. But as this normally measures relative prices by the real effective exchange rate based on the consumer price index, and the demand for exports depends on trade prices (production prices in the source country plus the costs of transporting the product to the other country), a reduced form equation includes aid to infrastructure and productive capacities because these types of aid affect the costs of trading via infrastructure and developing trade.

For example, better infrastructure, better marketing links or improved standards should make it easier to trade, but they tend to be excluded from traditional export and import demand equations:

$$Ln(E)_{it} = \alpha_i + \gamma_1 \ln(1 + Apc)_{it-1} + \gamma_2(1 + Ai)_{it-1} + KEZ_{it} + \lambda_t + \varepsilon_{it} \quad (2)$$

Where E is the volume of exports (country i, time t), Apc is aid for productive capacity and Ai is aid for economic infrastructure, α_i country effects, λ_t estimation period effects and Z a vector of controls, including relative prices and a measure of international demand.

Specification (1) has a number of potential problems that may bias the results, including omitted variable bias, owing to unobserved cross-country heterogeneity, and potential endogeneity of the AfT variable (e.g. if better reforming countries tend to receive more aid). Specification (2) is less subject to omitted variable bias than (1), as it controls for time invariant country characteristics (such as geography, location, and history). However, this specification still suffers to some extent from omitted variable bias of cross-country regressions due to time varying differences across countries.

To overcome these problems, we use a strategy based on inter-sectoral and intra-sectoral (over time) differences in exports. We divide aid to productive capacities into aid to the different sectors and then relate sectoral aid to sector-specific exports. This helps to identify whether sectors in the same country that receive more aid experience relatively faster growth in their exports (between group component), as well as whether exports of a sector grow faster in years in which that sector receives relatively higher levels of aid (within group component). The main advantage of this strategy is that it allows us to control for all time varying within country factors that may influence exports, such as effective demand, policies, size of the economy, economic fundamentals, country-level shocks, etc. Because of this, we can also use value of exports as the dependent variable instead of real exports (as in the specification (2)), which allows us to have more observations. We use four large sectors of the economy for which export data (from the World Development Indicators) are available: food production, manufacturing, mineral extraction and tourism. These account for all exports of goods and part of services exports of the countries in the panel. We match these sectors with their counterparts in the aid data: agriculture and fishing, industry, mining and tourism.

We estimate the following equation:

$$\ln X_{ijt} = \alpha_{it} + \delta_1 \ln Apc_{ijt-1} + \delta_2 \ln(Apc_{ijt-1})^2 = \phi\Delta \ln X_{ijt-1} + \lambda_{jt} + \varepsilon_{ijt} \quad (3)$$

where X is the value of exports (for country i, sector j and time t), Apc is aid to productive capacity, α_{ij} is country-year fixed effects, λ_{jt} is time varying sector fixed effects and ΔX is the proportionate rate of growth of exports in country i and sector j in the previous period. The latter variable serves to control for the endogeneity of aid, i.e. if aid for productive capacity may also be allocated on the basis of the growth of exports.

Data

We employ data from a variety of sources. Aid data is taken from the OECD CRS database on disbursements. This database has covered a number of AfT activities since the mid-1970s; reporting to the CRS is improving and improvements are being made to the data. We use different types of AfT data from this database, including aid for trade policy and regulations, aid to productive capacity (both total and sectoral) and aid for economic infrastructure. These categories, as well as the basic structure of the database, are described in Box 3.1. We have also used the WTO/OECD (2008) database for trade facilitation data. This was a joint effort by the OECD and WTO, and covered a large number of trade-related technical assistance projects between 2001 and 2006.[8] As the OECD CRS is likely to become the standard for aid for trade data collection, we use data from WTO/OECD only for robustness checks.

Data on investment climate indicators have become available for a large number of

Box 3.1. Aid for Trade data in the OECD CRS database

The OECD Development Co-operation Directorate bases its classification of the destinations of aid on the specific area of the social or economic structure in the receiving country that the aid transfer is intended to foster. The categories therefore refer to the overarching goal (e.g. trade facilitation), rather than the service provided through the funds (e.g. funding of regional trade agreements (RTAs) or training). The system of purpose codes summarises this classification in five digits: the first three refer to the respective DAC5 sector, and the remaining two represent numbering from more general (10–50) to more specific (60–90).

- ***Ainf*** *Economic Infrastructure*, coded as number 200, includes transport and storage, communications, energy, banking and financial services, and business and other services, each with its own sub-components.
- ***Apc*** *Production sectors*, coded as 300, includes the four sectors treated separately: agriculture-forestry-fishing, industry-mining-construction, trade policy and regulations, and tourism.
- ***Atpr*** *Trade Policy and Regulations*, coded as 331, is composed of trade policy and administrative management, trade facilitation, regional trade agreements, multilateral trade negotiations, trade-related adjustment and trade education/training. The same holds true for tourism, which has only one final component: tourism policy and administrative management.

The other destinations for sectoral aid for productive capacity all have multiple ramifications and are further focused. Under the category agriculture-forestry-fishing, *agriculture* (coded 311) has 18 final components, ranging from the general agricultural policy and administrative management (31110) to specific livestock/veterinary services (31195). The same applies for *fishing* (313), which incorporates five possible destinations for aid. The category industry-mining-construction has among its sub-sections *industry* (321) and *mineral resources and mining* (322), which we use for proxying aid to manufacturing and minerals sectors respectively in the analysis below.

Source: OECD CRS website; see also Turner (2008)

countries through the World Bank report, *Doing Business*. These surveys cover the number of documents, and the time and costs required to change a certain regulation (e.g. in relation to registering property or dealing with licences). We focus on indicators for trade across borders provided in *Doing Business* (see Appendix 1). For total export data, we construct real exports series using IMF (2008) data on values and unit values, and we extract sectoral export data (in current US$) from World Bank (2008). We also use the real effective exchange rate from the IMF (2008) and the volume of world imports or GDP from World Bank (2008).

4

Empirical Results

Aid for Trade and the costs of trading

Principal results

Table 4.1 presents the estimation results of the equation for costs of trading (exporting first) in 2008. We focus on this variable because it has an obvious relation to trade, but it is straightforward from a statistical point of view to examine some other indicators as well. The costs of trading variables are not particularly suitable for constructing time series due to data availability, so we focus on one year. We estimate equation (1) for a cross-section of around 120 developing countries.

There are a number of important findings. Aid to productive capacities (*Atpr*) has a mildly negative effect on the costs of exporting, but is not significant when it is used in a parsimonious specification with only the total size of the economy as a control (column 1). The results are not in line with expectations, but they are not surprising given the way the cost index is constructed. The index includes the official costs for transport from the factory to the point of departure. These are likely to be much larger for a factory situated in a landlocked country. The small effect of *Atpr* on that specification is probably because of omitted variable bias, as its coefficient becomes larger and highly significant (at the 1 per cent level) when other important variables relating to costs of exporting are added (column 2). These include a good governance indicator, which reduces costs of exporting, income per capita, which reduces costs of X, although it is not significant, and a dummy for being landlocked, which significantly increases the cost of exporting.

The coefficient of the size of the economy remains negative, but becomes insignificant in column 2. This suggests that the cost-reducing effect recorded in column 1 was probably due to that variable capturing a negative effect of income per capita (which is an indicator of better governance indicators). The cost reduction associated with an increase of 1 per cent in *Atpr* is considerable at around 0.136 per cent of the costs of exporting. Put differently, an increase of US$15,000 in *Atpr* (from the mean of US$1.48 million) is associated with a reduction of US$1.80 (from the mean of US$1324) in the costs of packing goods and loading them into a 20-foot container, transporting them to the port of departure and loading them on the vessel or truck.

The results for column 2 may be biased due to reverse causality if, for example, more efficient procedures for handling exports lead to countries receiving more *Atpr*.[9] To deal with this issue, we include in the regression the costs of exporting index lagged one year (for 2007) (see column 3). The coefficient of *Atpr* remains highly significant to this addition and it is the only variable which does not experience a reduction in its level of significance. These results are also robust to the restriction of the sample to countries for

Table 4.1. Explaining costs of exports (1n of US$ per container in 2008)

Sample	(1) All	(2) All	(3) All	(4) *Tpr*06>0	(5) All	(6) All	(7) Africa	(8) Africa	(9) All
Aid for trade policy and regulation									
$\log(1+TPR)_{2006}$	−0.062	−0.136	−0.089	−0.109	−0.080	−0.085	−0.072	−0.040	
	(1.01)	(2.83)[c]	(2.60)[b]	(2.82)[c]	(1.90)[a]	(1.76)[a]	(2.11)[b]	(0.75)	
$\log(1+\text{avg } TPR)_{2005\text{–}06}$									−0.075
									(2.33)[b]
Log GDP_{2006}	−0.053	−0.013	0.017	0.025	0.016	0.018	0.005	0.002	0.015
	(2.53)[b]	(0.63)	(1.52)	(1.75)[a]	(1.38)	(1.34)	(0.25)	(0.12)	(1.32)
Governance_{2006}		−0.173	−0.062	−0.070	−0.063	−0.063	0.014	0.004	−0.067
		(2.29)[b]	(1.18)	(1.09)	(1.21)	(1.27)	(0.42)	(0.11)	(1.26)
Log GNI per capita_{2004}		−0.040	−0.004	−0.005	−0.002	−0.005	−0.042	−0.033	0.002
		(0.94)	(0.14)	(0.17)	(0.07)	(0.22)	(1.57)	(1.05)	(0.09)
Landlocked		0.489	0.090	0.116	0.090	0.100	0.109	0.112	0.097
		(5.19)[c]	(1.88)[a]	(1.83)[a]	(1.87)[a]	(1.70)	(1.01)	(1.02)	(1.93)[a]
$\log(X\text{ cost})_{2007}$			0.837	0.816	0.839	0.830	0.878	0.881	0.841
			(13.90)[c]	(11.11)[c]	(13.59)[c]	(11.79)[c]	(8.62)[c]	(8.45)[c]	(14.07)[c]
Egypt					−0.120	−0.110		−0.201	
					(1.04)	(0.81)		(1.30)	
Asia						−0.028			
						(0.71)			
America						0.024			
						(0.40)			
Europe						−0.050			
						(0.50)			
Constant	7.208	7.255	1.143	1.295	1.114	1.202	1.152	1.057	1.072

Table 4.1 (continued)

Sample	(1) **All**	(2) **All**	(3) **All**	(4) ***Tpr*06>0**	(5) **All**	(6) **All**	(7) **Africa**	(8) **Africa**	(9) **All**
Observations	129	120	119	97	119	119	49	49	119
R-squared	0.07	0.42	0.86	0.85	0.86	0.86	0.90	0.90	0.86

Robust t-statistics in parentheses; [a]significant at 10 per cent; [b]significant at 5 per cent; [c]significant at 1 per cent; dependent variable is 1n(1+cost of exporting)$_{2008}$.

which a positive value of *Atpr* is reported (column 4). This robustness check is important to verify that results are not driven by potential misreporting. That would be the case if, for instance, countries which appear not to have received any *Atpr* are in fact just non-reporting countries. The cost-reducing effect of *Atpr* holds also when a dummy for Egypt (by far the largest *Atpr* recipient in our sample) is included, and dummies for the main continents (columns 5 and 6).[10] The effect of *Atpr* in Africa is slightly lower than for the whole sample (column 7), and it appears to be mainly driven by Egypt (column 8). If Egypt is included as an additional variable, *Atpr* does not have a significant effect. This calls for a closer evaluation of the effects of this type of aid on African countries. Finally, the results are robust to the use of the average value of *Atpr* between 2005 and 2006, to excluding the possibility that cross-country year-to-year fluctuations of aid are not driving the findings (column 9). The high values of R-squared for columns 3–9 suggest that these regressions are well specified, explaining up to 86 per cent of the cross-country variability in the changes of the costs of exporting.

Figure 4.1 suggests that the negative relationship found in the regressions is not due to the presence of outliers or influential observations (Egypt is excluded from the picture).

Figure 4.1. Conditional relation between costs of exporting and *Atpr*

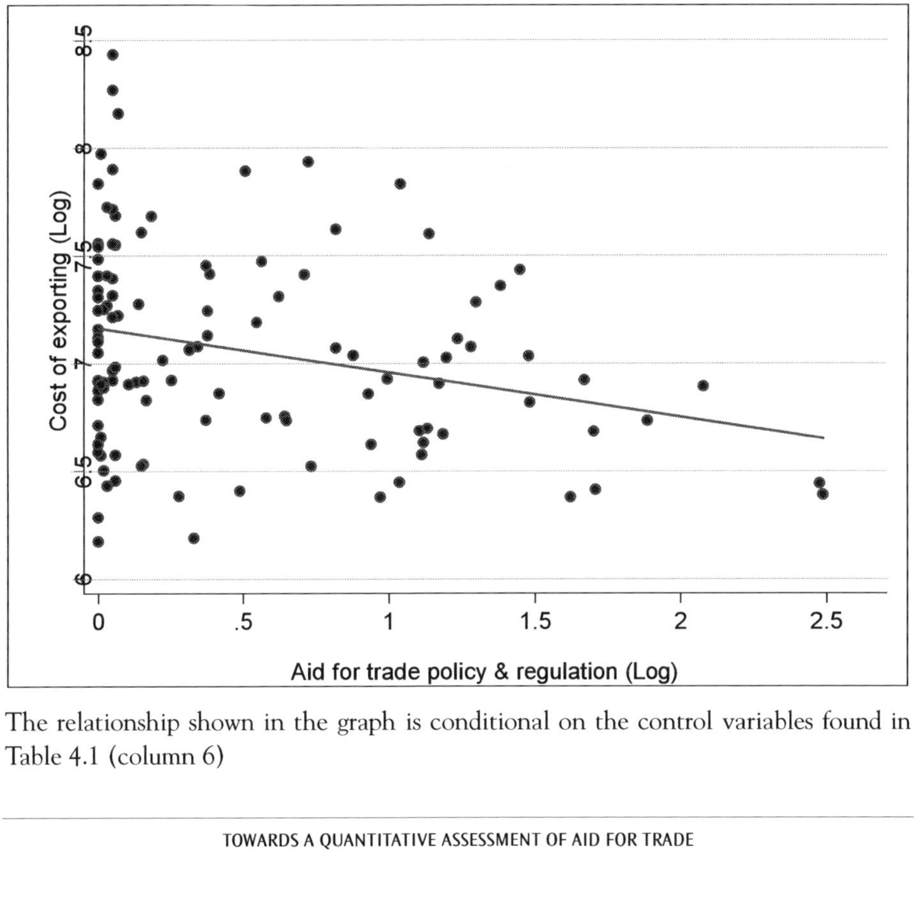

The relationship shown in the graph is conditional on the control variables found in Table 4.1 (column 6)

Costs of importing, and time of exporting and importing

We carried out additional tests to check whether our findings are robust to the use of other dependent variables as well as to other main regressors. Table 4.2 presents the results. The results of Table 4.1 hold when using costs of importing (rather than exporting) as the dependent variable (columns 1 and 2), and the coefficient of *Atpr* is very similar (only slightly smaller) than that of Table 4.1.

Higher *Atpr* is associated with decreases in the time taken to export goods (column 3). The results in column 4, where a control for the number of documents is added, suggest that this result is not driven by a lower number of documents to be processed. These results for time (to export) do not to apply to the same extent to dynamic specifications. Adding the time taken for exporting in 2007 (column 5) makes the coefficient of *Atpr* insignificant and reduces its value substantially (although it is still negative). This suggests that *Atpr* does not significantly affect changes in time to export, which is rather explained by other control variables, such as governance, the size of the economy and being landlocked. This case is confirmed in the case of Africa (column 6).

The negative effect of AfT on the costs of exporting is confirmed by the use of aid for trade facilitation (*Atf* a sub-category) in place of *Atpr*. Unlike the latter, this variable has a non-linear U-shaped relationship with the costs of exporting (as suggested by the difference in the coefficient's significance between column 7 and 8). This implies that *Atf* reduces the cost at a diminishing rate up to a trough, after which it even increases it. This is consistent with the idea of diminishing returns to aid already found by other studies (e.g. Hansen and Tarp, 2001; Clemens et al., 2004). This relationship is robust to restricting the sample to those countries which report positive levels of *Atpr* (column 9), but not when using the time of exports as the dependent variable (column 10). In the latter case the relation appears negative and linear, although not significant.[11]

Table 4.2. The effects of Aid for Trade on other trade cost variables

Dep var.	(1) Log (M cost)$_{2008}$	(2) Log (M cost)$_{2008}$	(3) Log (X time)$_{2008}$	(4) Log (X time)$_{2008}$	(5) Log (X time)$_{2008}$	(6) Log (X time)$_{2008}$	(7) Log (X cost)$_{2008}$	(8) Log (X cost)$_{2008}$	(9) Log (X cost)$_{2008}$	(10) Log (X time)$_{2008}$
Sample	All	All	All	All	All	Africa	All	All	*Tpr*06>0	All
Aid for trade policy and regulations										
Log (1+*Atpr*)$_{2006}$	−0.074	−0.078	−0.088	−0.082	−0.019	−0.014				
	(2.67)[c]	(2.54)[b]	(2.13)[b]	(2.02)[b]	(0.79)	(0.53)				
Aid for trade facilitation (narrow)										
Log (1 + *Atf*)$_{2006}$							−0.009	−0.047	−0.076	−0.010
							(0.87)	(1.68)[a]	(1.96)[a]	(1.42)
Log (1 + *Atf*)$_{2006}$ sq.								0.004	0.006	
								(1.60)	(1.99)[b]	
Log GDP$_{2006}$	0.011	0.012	0.015	0.011	−0.016	−0.007	0.008	0.010	0.021	−0.013
	(1.10)	(1.12)	(0.93)	(0.71)	(1.87)[a]	(0.63)	(0.74)	(0.92)	(1.35)	(1.73)[a]
Governance$_{2006}$	−0.045	−0.044	−0.160	−0.131	−0.063	−0.045	−0.075	−0.076	−0.084	−0.065
	(1.27)	(1.30)	(2.70)[c]	(2.20)[b]	(2.22)[b]	(1.22)	(1.26)	(1.27)	(1.20)	(2.00)[b]
Log GNI per capita$_{2004}$	−0.003	−0.005	−0.092	−0.089	0.037	0.007	0.009	0.007	0.007	0.032
	(0.20)	(0.36)	(2.53)[b]	(2.46)[b]	(1.90)	(0.63)	(0.36)	(0.26)	(0.22)	(1.53)
Landlocked	0.062	0.070	0.484	0.448	0.108	0.069	0.117	0.126	0.138	0.115
	(2.38)[b]	(2.38)[b]	(6.20)[c]	(5.64)[c]	(2.98)[c]	(1.49)	(1.76)[a]	(1.83)	(1.62)	(3.10)[c]
Log (M Cost)$_{2007}$	0.911	0.904								
	(29.63)[c]	(26.54)[c]								
Log (X time)$_{2007}$					0.851	0.881				0.851
					(14.30)[c]	(13.27)[c]				(13.96)[c]
Log (X Cost)$_{2007}$							0.836	0.833	0.815	
							(11.94)[c]	(11.76)[c]	(9.26)[c]	

Table 4.2 (continued)

Dep var. **Sample**	**(1)** **Log (M cost)$_{2008}$** **All**	**(2)** **Log (M cost)$_{2008}$** **All**	**(3)** **Log (X time)$_{2008}$** **All**	**(4)** **Log (X time)$_{2008}$** **All**	**(5)** **Log (X time)$_{2008}$** **All**	**(6)** **Log (X time)$_{2008}$** **Africa**	**(7)** **Log (X cost)$_{2008}$** **All**	**(8)** **Log (X cost)$_{2008}$** **All**	**(9)** **Log (X cost)$_{2008}$** **Tpr06>0**	**(10)** **Log (X time)$_{2C08}$** **All**
Log (*X* Docs)$_{2007}$				0.271 ((2.14)[b]	0.064 (1.19)	0.130 (1.52)				0.061 (1.13)
Asia		–0.011 (0.38)	0.056 (0.84)	0.048 (0.75)	0.003 (0.13)		–0.019 (0.52)	–0.016 (0.44)	–0.015 (0.34)	0.017 (0.61)
America		0.012 (0.25)	–0.087 (0.99)	–0.073 (0.87)	–0.023 (0.55)		0.021 (0.34)	0.031 (0.53)	0.012 (0.18)	–0.012 (0.29)
Europe		–0.041 (0.56)	–0.460 (2.39)[b]	–0.428 (2.16)[b]	–0.089 (1.26)		–0.000 (0.00)	–0.036 (0.32)	0.069 (0.30)	–0.080 (1.05)
Egypt						–0.292 (3.05)[c]			–0.358 (8.18)[c]	
Constant	0.637	0.698	3.791	3.255	0.083	0.053	1.061	1.172	1.356	0.139
Observations	119	119	120	120	119	49	118	118	97	118
R-squared	0.93	0.94	0.61	0.63	0.93	0.96	0.85	0.85	0.85	0.93

Robust t-statistics in parentheses; [a]significant at 10 per cent; [b]significant at 5 per cent; [c]significant at 1 per cent.

Aid for Trade and exports

Macro analysis

We use a standard export demand equation as in equation (2), where the volume of exports depends on relative prices and the demand for exports. We proxy these two variables through the Real Effective Exchange Rate (REER) and world GDP, respectively. We employ two aid measures: aid to economic infrastructure and aid to productive capacities.

Table 4.3 presents the results of the analysis. Aid for productive capacity (*Apc*) has an insignificant effect on real exports (column 1), while world demand is highly and positively related to real exports and REER has the expected negative sign but is not significant (column 1). When we re-run the same regression using year effects, the coefficient on aid for productive capacity becomes more negative and mildly significant, while the coefficient for REER is insignificant (column 2).

This negative result for *Apc* is driven by the restricted sample we are using (44 developing countries), which is constrained by the availability of REER data. Given the insignificance of the REER coefficient (which is also orthogonal to the aid variable), we drop it, and the *Apc* coefficient then becomes insignificant (column 3).

The effect of restricting the sample to countries for which REER data are available is even more distorting when we use aid to economic infrastructure (*Ainf*). With this restricted sample, this variable exerts an insignificant effect on exports (column 4); this positive effect becomes much larger (and the coefficient highly significant) when we use the full sample (column 5).

The impact of *Ainf* on exports appears to be highly non-linear U-shaped (column 6). This type of relationship is confirmed when both aid variables are included (column 7). In this case, *Apc* appears to exert a negative and significant impact on real exports, while *Ainf* has a negative and then a highly positive effect on exports. The latter effect may be explained through the lumpiness of the investment in economic infrastructure. If this investment is insufficient, the infrastructure would not reduce export prices and thus stimulate exports.

It is more difficult to explain the negative coefficient of *Apc*. It is possible that this effect is driven by omitted variable bias due to unobserved time varying heterogeneity across countries (e.g. specific country shocks) or by problems with the identification strategy, i.e. *Apc* has mainly sectoral effects and considering its impact on the whole of exports may be misleading. Of course it could also be the case that this type of aid is not actually spent effectively and actually harms exports via Dutch Disease type effects by subsidising inefficient production within the country.

The positive effects of aid to infrastructure are clearer for non-African countries than for African countries. These results are robust to the exclusion of country-year pairs for which a value of zero for both types of aid is reported (column 8). These effects appear to be magnified when world demand is higher (negative and significant effect for the interaction between *Apc* and world demand and positive and significant effect for the interaction between *Apc* and world demand (column 9)). Finally, the results for Africa

Table 4.3. Real exports and Aid for Trade (1984–2006)

Sample	(1) REER available	(2) REER available	(3) All	(4) REER available	(5) All	(6) All	(7) All	(8) *Ai* and *Apc*>0	(9) All	(10) Africa
Aid for productive capacities										
Log $(1+Apc)_{t-1}$	−0.025	−0.038	−0.007				−0.038	−0.049	0.354	−0.041
	(1.31)	(1.77)[a]	(0.54)				(2.74)[c]	(4.07)[c]	(2.13)[b]	(1.39)
Aid for infrastructure										
Log $(1+Ainfra)_{t-1}$				0.033	0.059	−0.131	−0.120	−0.169	−0.129	−0.121
				(1.35)	(4.00)[c]	(3.75)[c]	(3.34)[c]	(3.99)[c]	(3.96)[c]	(1.21)
Log $(1+Ainfra)_{t-1}$ sq.						0.035	0.035	0.026	−0.026	0.044
						(6.40)[c]	(6.55)[c]	(4.24)[c]	(0.81)	(1.86)[a]
Log REER	−0.017	−0.024		−0.012						
	(0.26)	(0.31)		(0.16)						
Log World GDP	1.242									
	(16.44)[c]									
Log $(1+Apc)_{t-1}$ x world GDP									−0.070	
									(2.29)[b]	
Log $(1+Ainfra)_{t-1}$ x world GDP									0.010	
									(1.87)[a]	
Constant	−2.670	4.922	4.261	4.696	4.144	4.225	4.190	5.247	2.864	3.514
Year effects	NO	YES	YES	YES	YES	YES	YES	YES	YES	YES
Country effects	YES	YES	YES	YES	YES	YES	YES	YES	YES	YES
Observations	466	497	1468	497	1468	1468	1468	457	1009	350
Number of countries	44	44	82	44	82	82	82	43	81	26
R-squared	0.48	0.49	0.53	0.49	0.54	0.55	0.55	0.71	0.59	0.47

Robust t-statistics in parentheses; [a]significant at 10 per cent; [b]significant at 5 per cent; [c]significant at 1 per cent are qualitatively in line with those of the whole sample but less robust (column 10). The most important findings are that different types of aid can have different effects and that these vary across regions.

Sectoral analysis

The surprising impact of *Apc* on exports suggests problems in the type of specification used to estimate the equations in Table 4.3. In order to deal with these issues, we adopt the specifications based on equation (3), analysing the impact of sectoral aid on sectoral exports. We study how the inter-sectoral, as well as intra-sectoral (over time), variation in aid and exports is related, using data from four sectors: food production, manufacturing, mineral extraction and tourism.

The results are clear and show a robust, positive and non-linear effect of *Apc* on exports. In line with the results shown in Table 4.2, as well as with other findings on the impact of aid on growth (e.g. Hansen and Tarp, 2001; Clemens et al., 2004), this relationship has the shape of an inverted U. Aid has a positive impact on exports at a diminishing rate.

These results are robust to a variety of specifications, control variables and sampling strategies. Tables 4.4 and 4.5 show that they are robust to the inclusion of country and sector-year fixed effects (columns 1–3), country-year fixed effects only (column 4) and both country-year and sector-year fixed effects (columns 5–13). They are also robust to using different types of samples: including only observations with positive values of *Apc*; including all observations (columns 7 and 8); and including only years after 1990 (columns 6 and 7). The power of the results also holds when including a lagged change in export variables (which has a highly negative association with the dependent variable). This controls for a potential source of endogeneity in aid allocation, as discussed above. Moreover, *Apc* also has a positive (although only at 10 per cent) impact on the rate of export growth (column 11, where a lagged export variable is included). The effect of *Apc* is around 50 per cent larger when country-year fixed effects are included, instead of only country effects (see columns 1 and 5), confirming that time varying country-specific effects (e.g. policies, shocks and state of the economy) play an important conditioning role in determining the impact of aid on exports.

There are a number of other interesting findings from the regressions reported in Tables 4.4 and 4.5. First, aid to economic infrastructure appears to exert a positive and significant effect on exports (columns 2–3). Such an effect is linear, unlike that found in regression (2) and reported in Table 4.3.[12] Moreover, *Ainf* appears to interact with *Apc* in affecting exports in a non-linear way (columns 10 and 12). *Apc* has a smaller positive impact for higher levels of *Ainf*, although the effect of this interaction changes as *Apc* increases, becoming positive for high levels of *Apc*. This suggests that positive complementarities between these two types of aid tend to emerge for relatively large amounts of *Apc*. Such complementarities appear to be positive in the case of landlocked economies (column 12).

Table 4.4. Sectoral exports and sectoral aid for productive capacity (1985–2006)

Sample	(1) *Apc*>0	(2) *Apc*>0	(3) *Apc*>0	(4) *Apc*>0	(5) *Apc*>0	(6) *Apc*>0 and post-1990	(7) post-1990
Aid for productive capacities							
Log $(1+Apc)_{t-1}$	0.446	0.438	0.423	0.624	0.658	0.710	0.629
	(7.93)[c]	(7.75)[c]	(8.58)[c]	(8.23)[c]	(8.21)[c]	(8.62)[c]	(8.72)[c]
Log $(1+Apc)_{t-1}$ sq.	–0.049	-0.048	-0.050	-0.071	-0.073	-0.078	-0.090
	(4.14)[c]	(4.09)[c]	(4.72)[c]	(4.38)[c]	(4.28)[c]	(4.58)[c]	(5.67)[c]
Aid for infrastructure		0.055	0.035				
Log $(1+Ainf)_{t-1}$		(2.74)[c]	(1.75)[a]				
Manufacturing				0.646			
				(11.11)[c]			
Minerals				–1.120			
				(9.68)[c]			
Tourism				0.561			
				(5.73)[c]			
Δ $Export_{t-1}$			–0.030				
			(6.02)[c]				
Country effects	YES	YES	YES				
Country-year effects	NO	NO	NO	YES	YES	YES	YES
Sector-year effects	YES	YES	YES	NO	YES	YES	YES
Constant	16.701	16.659	17.958	19.129	18.549	18.494	18.721
Observations	3647	3595	3167	3647	3647	3340	6176
R-squared	0.79	0.79	0.81	0.84	0.84	0.83	0.79

Robust t-statistics in parentheses; [a]significant at 10 per cent; [b]significant at 5 per cent; [c]significant at 1 per cent; dependent variable is log of export value (in current US$).

The effects of *Apc* are relatively more important in supporting exports in mining and manufacturing than in tourism and agriculture (column 13). This suggests that the more capital-intensive sectors (such as mining and manufacturing) are also the ones where the lack of domestic resources has been most penalising in developing countries. Aid can thus play a role helping to move the comparative advantage of (certain) developing countries away from non-capital intensive sectors.

Table 4.5. Sectoral exports and aid for productive capacity, developing countries (1985–2006)

Sample	(8) All	(9) *Apc*>0	(10) *Apc*>0	(11) *Apc*>0	(12) *Apc*>0	(13) *Apc*>0
Aid for productive capacities						
$\text{Log}(1+Apc)_{t-1}$	0.492	0.622	0.976	0.033	0.614	0.480
	(7.16)[c]	(8.55)[c]	(5.77)[c]	(1.89)[a]	(3.74)[c]	(2.78)[c]
$\text{Log}(1+Apc)_{t-1}$ sq.	–0.068	–0.072	–0.156		–0.167	–0.060
	(4.47)[c]	(4.54)[c]	(3.39)[c]		(3.87)[c]	(1.34)
Δ Export_{t-1}		–0.038			–0.038	
		(6.10)[c]			(5.93)[c]	
$(Apc \times Ainf)_{t-1}$			–0.081	–0.006	–0.076	–0.034
			(2.31)[b]	(0.99)	(2.32)[b]	(1.00)
$(Apc \text{ sq.} \times Ainf)_{t-1}$			0.020	0.000	0.023	–0.004
			(2.31)[b]	(0.53)	(2.88)[c]	(0.51)
$\text{Log (export)}_{t-1}$				0.948		
				(62.50)[c]		
Apc x *Ainf* x landlocked					0.069	
					(3.65)[c]	
Apc x America					0.381	
					(4.02)[c]	
Apc x Asia and Oceania					0.201	
					(2.07)[b]	
Apc x Africa					0.280	
					(2.84)[c]	
Apc x Mineral						0.436
						(4.13)[c]
Apc x Manufacturing						0.380
						(8.18)[c]
Apc x Tourism						–0.060
						(0.57)
Country-year effects	YES	YES	YES	YES	YES	YES
Sector-year effects	YES	YES	YES	YES	YES	YES
Constant	18.220	18.807	18.931	1.095	18.820	19.176
Observations	9963	3216	3595	3375	3167	3595
R-squared	0.77	0.85	0.84	0.98	0.85	0.84

Robust t-statistics in parentheses; [a]significant at 10 per cent; [b]significant at 5 per cent; [c]significant at 1 per cent; dependent variable is log of export value (in current US$).

5

Policy Implications and Future Research

This paper has a number of key findings. We have argued that Aid for Trade should affect trade directly or indirectly by improving the investment climate in which trade takes place. We found that AfT can have a positive effect on investment climate indicators. We found that AfT that falls into the category of trade policy and regulations has helped to reduce the costs of trading, controlling for a number of other factors such as governance generally, being landlocked and income status. This is a key policy finding because it shows that AfT is effective where it aims to be effective (subject, of course, to the quality of reporting by donors to the OECD CRS database).

The results are clear and show that *Apc* has a robust, positive and non-linear effect on exports. In line with the results shown in Table 4.2, as well as with other findings on the impact of aid on growth (e.g. Hansen and Tarp, 2001; Clemens et al., 2004), this relationship has the shape of an inverted U. Aid has a positive impact on exports at a diminishing rate. The second finding is that it is more difficult to establish a direct relationship between AfT, especially aid to productive capacity, and total exports. We have undertaken a number of regressions which tend to suggest that different types of aid affect exports differently, hence the difficulty in finding an aggregate effect in the literature. But on closer inspection, it seems that aid to productive capacity must be modelled by sector, while aid to infrastructure has a positive or negative effect depending on empirical specifications.

To overcome this problem, we employ a new strategy based on inter-sectoral and intra-sectoral (over time) differences in exports. We divide aid to productive capacities into aid to the different sectors and then relate sectoral aid to sectoral exports. The identification comes from analysing whether sectors that receive more aid relative to other sectors in the same country experience relatively faster growth in their exports (between group component), as well as whether exports of a sector grew faster in years in which that sector received a relatively high level of aid (within group component). The main advantage of this strategy is that it allows us to control for all time varying country factors which may influence exports, such as effective demand, policies, size of the economy, economic fundamentals, country-level shocks, etc. The results based on this new identification strategy are clear and show there is a robust, positive and non-linear effect of *Apc* on exports.

The paper examines other aid categories and new dependent variables. There are a number of policy implications:

- There are a number of pathways through which AfT affects trade;
- AfT has significant and measurable effects in reducing the cost of trading, which is an important investment climate indicator relevant to exporting;

- While the effects of AfT on exports are more ambivalent depending on the specification used, when properly specified, AfT does foster exports in productive sectors, up to a point;
- Aid for infrastructure has significant positive effects at both macro and sectoral level;
- Aid for Africa (if Egypt is excluded) has smaller, and sometimes insignificant, results.

The paper extends the literature on aid and growth by showing that refining the aid category into sub-groups related to AfT and examining effects at a more disaggregated level yields significant results. It started the impact assessment of trade-related aid using a number of outcome variables, as well as different measures of aid. Many extensions of the analysis are possible based on available data, which may bring about further insights into the effects of different types and modalities of aid on different countries, regions and variables. We propose some of these extensions below.

1. One possible extension could be to run a similar analysis to that in Table 4.1, but with panel data to control for country-specific time invariant effects. This would make estimation of the cost-effectiveness of this type of aid more precise.
2. It would also be possible to examine the effects of aid on specific regions and countries, performing the analysis in equation 3 on a subset of countries, such as small islands, landlocked economies, Africa, ACP countries or LDCs, and also on countries which differ in terms of economic specialisation. The methodology described in section 2 is robust enough to also extract consistent policy implications on fairly small subsets of countries. This is important, given the apparently varying effects.
3. Provided that the data in the OECD CRS database do not suffer from classification error at fairly disaggregated levels, we could slice the data further by purpose code and examine the effects of different types of specific trade-related aid on the investment climate and exports.
4. We could examine the impact of AfT on other types of dependent variables, such as the real exchange rate, to test whether and to what extent this aid can prevent Dutch disease type effects.
5. There is a need for more analysis and data on the 'trading climate' so that the type of analysis set out in this paper does not need to rely on data collected for investment analysis.

References

Adam, C and Bevan, DL (2006). 'Aid and the Supply Side: Public Investment, Export Performance, and Dutch Disease in Low-Income Countries', *World Bank Economic Review*, 20(2): 261–90.

Bourguignon, F and Sundberg, M (2007). 'Aid Effectiveness – Opening the Black Box', *American Economic Review*, 97(2): 316–21.

Burnside, C and Dollar, D (2000). 'Aid, policies, and growth', *American Economic Review*, 90 (4): 847–68.

Buys, P, Deichmann, U and Wheeler, D (2006). 'Road Network Upgrading and Overland Trade Expansion in Sub-Saharan Africa', mimeo, World Bank, Washington, DC.

Calì, M (2007). 'How reliable is the OECD/WTO database on Aid for Trade?', mimeo, ODI, London.

Calì, M, Grimm, S, Page, S, Phillips, L and DW te Velde (2006), 'The financial architecture of aid for trade', ILEAP Background Brief No. 9, International Lawyers and Economists Against Poverty, Toronto.

Canning, D (1998). 'A database of world infrastructure stock, 1960–95, mimeo, Harvard Institute for International Development, Cambridge, Mass.

Canning, D, Fay, M and Perotti, R (1994). 'Infrastructure and Growth', In Baldassarri, M, Paganetto, L and Phelps, E (eds), *International Differences in Growth Rates*, Macmillan Press Ltd, London and Basingstoke.

Clemens M, Radelet, S and Bhavnani, R (2004). 'Counting Chickens When They Hatch: The Short-term Effect of Aid on Growth', Working Paper 44, Center for Global Development, Washington, DC.

Doucouliagos, H, and Paldam, M (2007). *The Aid Effectiveness Literature. The Sad Result of 40 Years of Research*, Department of Economics Working Paper 2007–15, University of Aarhus, Aarhus, Denmark.

Djankov, S, Freund, C and Pham, CF (2006). 'Trading on time', Policy Research Working Paper 3909, World Bank, Washington, DC.

François, J and Manchin, M (2007). 'Institutions, Infrastructure and Trade,' Policy Research Working Paper 4152, World Bank, Washington, DC.

Gomanee, K, Girma, S and Morrissey, O (2002). 'Aid, Investment and Growth in Sub-Saharan Africa', paper prepared for the 10th General Conference of EADI, Ljubljana.

Hansen, H and Tarp, F (2001). 'Aid and Growth Regressions', *Journal of Development Economics*, 64: 547–70.

IMF (2008). *Direction of Trade Statistics*, CD-Rom.

Kaufmann, D, Kraay, A and Mastruzzi, M (2007). *Governance Matter VI: Governance Indicators 1996–2006*, World Bank, Washington, DC.

McPherson, MF and Rakowski, T (2001). 'Understanding the Growth Process in Sub-

Saharan Africa: Some Empirical Estimates', African Economic Policy Discussion Paper, Harvard University, Cambridge, Mass.

Radelet, S and Sachs, J (1999). 'Shipping costs, manufactured exports and economic growth', paper presented at the American Economic Association Meetings.

Rajan, RG and Subramanian, A (2005). 'What Undermines Aid's Impact on Growth?', IMF Working Paper 126, Washington, DC.

Rajan, RG and Subramanian, A (2007). 'Aid and Growth: What Does the Cross-Country Evidence Really Show?' (forthcoming).

Turner, L (2008). 'Quantifying Aid for Trade', draft paper for Commonwealth Secretariat, London.

Velde, DW te (2008). 'Financing International Public Goods A Framework to Address Aid for Trade' in Njinkeu, D and Cameron, H (eds), *Aid for Trade and Development*, Oxford University Press, Oxford.

Velde, DW te, Calì, M, Page, S and Hewitt, A (2006). 'A Critical Assessment of the EU's Trade-Related Assistance to Third Countries', report for the European Parliament, ODI, London.

World Bank (2008). *World Development Indicators 2008*, CD-Rom.

WTO (2006). *Aid for Trade Task Force: Recommendations of the Task Force on Aid for Trade*, WT/AFT/1, WTO, Geneva.

WTO/OECD (2008). Trade Capacity Building Database, available at: http://tcbdb.wto.org/

Appendix 1
Defining 'Trading Across Borders'

(taken from http://www.doingbusiness.org/MethodologySurveys/TradingAcrossBorders.aspx)

Doing Business compiles procedural requirements for exporting and importing a standardised cargo of goods by ocean transport. Every official procedure for exporting and importing the goods is recorded – from the contractual agreement between the two parties to the delivery of goods – along with the time and cost necessary for completion. All documents required for clearance of the goods across the border are also recorded. For exporting goods, procedures range from packing the goods at the factory to their departure from the port of exit. For importing goods, procedures range from the vessel's arrival at the port of entry to the cargo's delivery at the factory warehouse. Payment is made by letter of credit.

Local freight forwarders, shipping lines, customs brokers and port officials provide information on required documents and cost as well as the time to complete each procedure. To make the data comparable across countries, several assumptions about the business and the traded goods are used. Since 2007, assumptions have been refined to adjust for particularities of landlocked countries and reduce variations related to documentation involving private parties. In the case of landlocked countries, any port-related data are based on information provided by the relevant sea port country. Inland transport costs are based on number of kilometres. Any documentation between the shipper and trader is excluded.

Assumptions about the business

- A business with 100 or more employees
- Is located in the country's most populous city
- Is a private, limited liability company; it does not operate within an export processing zone or an industrial estate with special export or import privileges
- Is domestically owned with no foreign ownership
- Exports more than 10 per cent of its sales.

Assumptions about the traded goods

The traded product travels in a dry-cargo, 20-foot, full container load. The product:

- Is not hazardous nor does it include military items
- Does not require refrigeration or any other special environment

- Does not require any special phytosanitary or environmental safety standards other than accepted international standards.

Measuring documents required to export and import

All documents required to export and import the goods are recorded. It is assumed that the contract has already been agreed upon and signed by both parties. Documents include bank documents, customs declaration and clearance documents, port filing documents, import licenses and other official documents exchanged between the concerned parties. Documents filed simultaneously are considered different documents but with the same time frame for completion.

Measuring time required to import and export

Time is recorded in calendar days. The time calculation for a procedure starts from the moment it is initiated and runs until it is completed. If a procedure can be accelerated for an additional cost, the fastest legal procedure is chosen. It is assumed that neither the exporter nor the importer wastes time and that each commits to completing each remaining procedure without delay. Procedures that can be completed in parallel are measured as simultaneous. The waiting time between procedures – for example, during unloading of the cargo – is included in the measure.

Measuring costs required to import and export

Cost measures the fees levied on a 20-foot container in US$. All the fees associated with completing the procedures to export or import the goods are included. These include costs for documents, administrative fees for customs clearance and technical control, terminal handling charges and inland transport. The cost measure does not include tariffs or trade taxes. Only official costs are recorded.

Appendix 2

Doing Business 'Trading Across Borders'

Table A1. Trading across borders (sorted by costs of exporting)

Region or economy	Documents for export (number)	Time for export (days)	Costs of exporting (US$ per container)	Documents for import (number)	Time for import (days)	Costs of importing (US$ per container)
East Asia and Pacific	6.9	24.5	885.3	7.5	25.8	1,014.50
Eastern Europe and Central Asia	7	29.3	1,393.40	8.3	30.8	1,551.40
Latin America and Caribbean	7	22.2	1,107.50	7.6	25.8	1,228.40
Middle East and North Africa	7.1	24.8	992.2	8	28.7	1,128.90
OECD	4.5	9.8	905	5	10.4	986.1
South Asia	8.6	32.5	1,179.90	9.1	32.1	1,417.90
Sub-Saharan Africa	8.1	35.6	1,660.10	9	43.7	1,985.90
Afghanistan	12	67	2,500	11	71	2,100
Albania	7	21	745	9	22	750
Algeria	8	17	1,198	9	23	1,378
Angola	12	64	1,850	9	58	2,325
Antigua and Barbuda	5	19	1,107	6	19	1,174
Argentina	9	16	1,325	7	20	1,825
Armenia	7	30	1,165	8	24	1,335
Australia	6	9	930	6	12	1,120
Austria	4	8	843	5	8	843
Azerbaijan	9	56	2,715	14	56	2,945
Bangladesh	7	28	844	9	32	1,148
Belarus	8	24	1,672	8	29	1,672
Belgium	4	8	1,600	5	9	1,600
Belize	7	23	1,800	6	26	2,130
Benin	7	34	1,167	7	41	1,202
Bhutan	8	38	1,150	11	38	2,080
Bolivia	8	24	1,110	7	36	1,230
Bosnia and Herzegovina	6	19	1,030	7	18	985
Botswana	6	33	2,328	9	43	2,595
Brazil	8	18	1,090	7	22	1,240
Brunei	6	28	515	6	19	590
Bulgaria	5	23	1,329	7	21	1,377
Burkina Faso	11	45	2,096	11	54	3,522
Burundi	9	47	2,147	10	71	3,705
Cambodia	11	37	722	11	46	852
Cameroon	9	27	907	8	33	1,529
Canada	3	7	1,385	4	11	1,425
Cape Verde	5	21	1,024	5	21	1,024
Central African Republic	8	57	4,581	18	66	4,534
Chad	6	78	4,867	9	102	5,520
Chile	6	21	645	7	21	685
China	7	21	390	6	24	430

Table A1 (continued)

Region or economy	Documents for export (number)	Time for export (days)	Costs of exporting (US$ per container)	Documents for import (number)	Time for import (days)	Costs of importing (US$ per container)
Colombia	6	24	1,440	8	20	1,440
Comoros	10	30	971	10	21	974
Congo, Dem. Rep.	8	46	2,307	9	66	2,183
Congo, Rep.	11	50	2,201	12	62	2,201
Costa Rica	7	18	660	8	25	660
Côte d'Ivoire	10	23	1,653	8	43	2,457
Croatia	7	22	1,200	8	16	1,200
Czech Republic	5	16	775	7	18	860
Denmark	4	5	540	3	5	540
Djibouti	8	22	960	6	18	960
Dominica	7	16	1,197	8	18	1,107
Dominican Republic	6	12	815	7	13	1,015
Ecuador	10	22	1,090	8	44	1,090
Egypt	6	15	714	7	18	729
El Salvador	8	21	540	11	18	540
Equatorial Guinea	7	29	1,403	7	46	1,403
Eritrea	9	59	1,331	13	69	1,581
Estonia	3	5	675	4	5	675
Ethiopia	8	46	1,617	8	42	2,793
Fiji Islands	13	25	573	13	25	570
Finland	4	8	420	5	8	420
France	4	11	1,028	5	12	1,148
Gabon	6	19	1,510	7	35	1,600
Gambia	7	23	809	8	23	869
Georgia	8	12	1,105	7	14	1,105
Germany	4	7	740	5	7	765
Ghana	6	19	895	7	29	895
Greece	5	20	998	6	25	1,245
Grenada	6	19	820	5	23	1,178
Guatemala	11	19	1,052	11	18	1,177
Guinea	7	33	570	9	32	995
Guinea-Bissau	6	27	1,445	6	26	1,749
Guyana	7	30	850	8	35	856
Haiti	8	52	1,650	10	53	1,860
Honduras	7	20	1,065	11	23	975
Hong Kong, China	4	6	525	4	5	525
Hungary	5	18	975	7	17	975
Iceland	5	15	469	5	14	443
India	8	18	820	9	21	910
Indonesia	5	21	667	6	27	623
Iran	8	26	860	10	42	1,330
Iraq	10	102	3,400	10	101	3,400
Ireland	4	7	1,090	4	12	1,139
Israel	5	12	560	4	12	560

Table A1 (continued)

Region or economy	Documents for export (number)	Time for export (days)	Costs of exporting (US$ per container)	Documents for import (number)	Time for import (days)	Costs of importing (US$ per container)
Italy	5	20	1,291	5	18	1,291
Jamaica	6	21	1,750	6	22	1,350
Japan	4	10	989	5	11	1,047
Jordan	7	19	680	7	22	1,065
Kazakhstan	12	89	2,730	14	76	2,780
Kenya	9	29	1,955	8	37	1,995
Kiribati	6	21	1,550	7	21	1,550
Korea	4	11	745	6	10	745
Kuwait	8	20	935	11	20	935
Kyrgyz Republic	13	64	2,500	13	75	2,450
Lao PDR	9	50	1,750	10	50	1,930
Latvia	6	13	800	6	12	800
Lebanon	5	27	1,027	7	38	810
Lesotho	6	44	1,188	8	49	1,210
Liberia	10	20	1,032	9	10	1,032
Lithuania	6	10	820	6	13	980
Luxembourg	5	6	1,250	4	6	1,250
Macedonia, FYR	7	19	1,130	7	17	1,130
Madagascar	4	28	1,182	10	49	1,282
Malawi	12	45	1,623	10	54	2,500
Malaysia	7	18	432	7	14	385
Maldives	8	21	1,200	9	20	1,200
Mali	9	44	1,752	11	65	2,680
Marshall Islands	5	21	765	5	33	765
Mauritania	11	35	1,360	11	42	1,363
Mauritius	5	17	728	6	16	673
Mexico	5	17	1,302	5	23	2,411
Micronesia	3	30	1,145	6	30	1,145
Moldova	6	32	1,425	7	35	1,545
Mongolia	10	58	1,807	10	59	3,197
Montenegro	9	18	1,580	7	19	1,780
Morocco	8	14	600	11	19	800
Mozambique	8	27	1,155	10	38	1,185
Namibia	11	29	1,539	9	24	1,550
Nepal	9	43	1,600	10	35	1,725
Netherlands	4	6	880	5	6	1,005
New Zealand	7	10	725	5	9	800
Nicaragua	5	36	1,021	5	38	1,054
Niger	8	59	2,945	10	68	2,946
Nigeria	10	26	1,026	9	46	1,047
Norway	4	7	518	4	7	468
Oman	10	22	665	10	26	824
Pakistan	9	24	515	8	19	1,336
Palau	6	29	1,160	10	35	1,110

Table A1 (continued)

Region or economy	Documents for export (number)	Time for export (days)	Costs of exporting (US$ per container)	Documents for import (number)	Time for import (days)	Costs of importing (US$ per container)
Panama	3	9	650	4	9	850
Papua New Guinea	7	26	584	9	29	642
Paraguay	9	35	720	10	33	900
Peru	7	24	590	8	31	670
Philippines	8	17	800	8	18	800
Poland	5	17	834	5	27	834
Portugal	6	16	580	7	16	994
Puerto Rico	7	15	1,225	10	16	1,225
Romania	5	12	1,075	6	13	1,075
Russia	8	36	2,050	13	36	2,050
Rwanda	9	47	2,975	9	69	4,970
Samoa	7	27	1,010	7	31	1,375
São Tomé and Principe	8	27	690	9	29	577
Saudi Arabia	5	19	1,008	5	20	758
Senegal	11	20	828	11	26	1,720
Serbia	6	12	1,240	6	14	1,440
Seychelles	6	17	1,839	5	19	1,839
Sierra Leone	8	31	1,282	7	34	1,242
Singapore	4	5	416	4	3	367
Slovakia	6	25	1,015	8	25	1,050
Slovenia	6	20	971	8	21	1,019
Solomon Islands	7	24	1,056	4	21	1,238
South Africa	8	30	1,087	9	35	1,195
Spain	6	9	1,000	8	10	1,000
Sri Lanka	8	21	810	6	21	844
St Kitts and Nevis	6	15	750	6	17	756
St Lucia	5	18	1,375	8	21	1,420
St Vincent and the Grenadines	6	15	1,770	6	16	1,769
Sudan	7	39	1,700	7	54	2,300
Suriname	8	25	905	7	25	815
Swaziland	9	21	1,798	11	34	1,820
Sweden	4	8	561	3	6	619
Switzerland	4	8	1,238	5	9	1,333
Syria	8	19	1,300	9	23	1,900
Taiwan, China	7	13	747	7	12	747
Tajikistan	10	82	3,000	11	83	4,500
Tanzania	5	24	1,212	7	30	1,425
Thailand	7	17	615	9	14	786
Timor-Leste	6	25	990	7	26	995
Togo	6	24	872	8	29	894
Tonga	7	19	545	6	25	620
Trinidad and Tobago	5	14	693	7	26	1,100
Tunisia	5	17	540	7	22	810
Turkey	7	14	865	8	15	1,013

Table A1 (continued)

Region or economy	Documents for export (number)	Time for export (days)	Costs of exporting (US$ per container)	Documents for import (number)	Time for import (days)	Costs of importing (US$ per container)
Uganda	6	39	2,940	7	37	2,990
Ukraine	6	31	1,045	10	39	1,065
United Arab Emirates	7	13	462	8	13	462
United Kingdom	4	13	940	4	13	1,267
United States	4	6	960	5	5	1,160
Uruguay	10	24	925	10	23	1,180
Uzbekistan	7	80	2,550	11	104	4,050
Vanuatu	7	26	1,815	9	30	2,225
Venezuela	8	45	2,400	9	65	2,400
Vietnam	6	24	669	8	23	881
West Bank and Gaza	6	25	830	6	40	995
Yemen	6	33	1,129	9	31	1,475
Zambia	8	53	2,098	11	64	2,840
Zimbabwe	9	52	1,879	13	67	2,420

Notes

1 For instance, we found large disparities between the AfT data recorded by the OECD/WTO and the AfT data as recorded by ministries in-country (Calì, 2007). The analysis also highlights the need for a better definition and a harmonisation of the categories used to record AfT, along with clear criteria on how to calculate the trade component in multipurpose projects. See also Turner (2008).

2 Te Velde et al. (2006) argue in relation to the evaluation of EC trade-related assistance activities: 'there is generally little quantitative evidence provided – descriptive or analytical – which is a significant gap. The EC's own assessment was based on interviews and analysis of documents, with no quantitative estimation of the impact of these activities on trade and economic development.'

3 WTO (2006).

4 See Burnside and Dollar (2000) and Rajan and Subramanian (2007) for illustrations.

5 The main results are robust to using ln (*Atpr*).

6 For instance, types of projects included in this category of aid include simplification and harmonisation of international import and export procedures (e.g. customs valuation, licensing procedures, transport formalities, payments, insurance) and support to customs departments.

7 We prefer to base the analysis on aid for trade policy and regulation data, rather than on aid for trade facilitation data for two reasons: first, the former encompasses a broader range of activities which may still be important in influencing the costs of trading across borders; second, the former data come from the OECD CRS database, which is likely to soon become the standard for aid for trade data (see below).

8 WTO/OECD reports on the WTO/OECD database and Calì et al. (2006) have discussed this database in detail to describe the pattern of past aid for trade spending by donors, recipients and category.

9 Such could be the case, for instance, if aid were allocated on the basis of the expected efficiency of its use (so that it would target relatively more efficient bureaucracies).

10 Oceania is included in Asia.

11 We test for nonlinearities, but the robust t-statistics for the coefficients of the linear and squared terms of *Aft* were 0.08 and 0.38 respectively (not reported here).

12 When we tried to include a squared term for *Ainf*, it made both terms jointly nonsignificant, according to an F-test.

Related titles from the Commonwealth Secretariat

Quantifying Aid for Trade: A Case Study of Tanzania
Liz Turner
Commonwealth Economic Paper Number 82, 2008

Using Tanzania as a case study Liz Turner shows how different definitions of Aid for Trade lead to different estimates of the amount being delivered. She suggests an alternative simple and practical methodology for recipient countries to classify and quantify it.

ISBN: 978-0-85092-888-4

Trading on Commonwealth Ties
Chris Milner
Commonwealth Economic Paper Number 79, 2008

What are the characteristics of current intra-Commonwealth trade, and how can it be encouraged to grow? *Trading on Commonwealth Ties* identifies opportunities for stimulating trade within the Commonwealth, and for boosting trade in general.

ISBN: 978-0-85092-875-4

Printed in Dunstable, United Kingdom

91343136R00027